The Avoidant Behavioral Condition

A Guide to Understanding, Managing and Treating Avoidant Personality Disorder and Helping a Loved one with AVPD

Ricky D. Coleman

Table of Contents

Chapter 1

UNDERSTANDING PERSONALITY DISORDERS/BEHAVIORAL CONDITIONS

What are Behavioral conditions?
Character is the way of reasoning, feeling, and acting that makes an individual unique about others. A person's character is affected by encounters, climate (environmental factors, life circumstances), and genetic characteristics. An individual's character frequently remains something similar over time.

A behavioral condition is a way of reasoning, feeling, and acting that veers off from the norms of the way of life, causes trouble or issues working, and endures after some time.

There are 10 explicit types of behavioral conditions. Behavioral conditions are long-haul examples of conduct and inside encounters that go astray emphatically based on what is generally anticipated. The example of involvement and direct conflict occurs during late youth or early adulthood and produces trouble or issues in working. Without treatment, behavioral conditions can long endure. Behavioral conditions impact no less than two of these areas:

- Perspective around oneself as well as other people

- Approach to answering sincerely

- Approach to connecting with others

- Approach to dealing with one's lead

Kinds of Behavioral conditions

Total disregard for other people: an example of dismissing or abusing the privileges of others. An individual with a total disregard for other people may not adjust to normal practices, may continually lie or bamboozle others, or may act hastily.

1. **<u>Avoidant behavioral condition/Avoidant personality disorder</u>**: This is also known as Avoidant personality disorder. An example of extreme modesty, serious insecurities, and intense aversion to analysis. Individuals with an avoidant behavioral condition might be hesitant to get drawn in with individuals except if they are sure of being preferred, are stressed over being censured or dismissed, or may see themselves as not being adequate or socially bumbling.

2. **<u>Marginal behavioral condition/Borderline personality disorder</u>**: an example of precariousness in private connections, high feelings, low mental self-portrait, and impulsivity. An individual with a marginal behavioral condition might go to huge endeavors to try not to be deserted, have rehashed self-destruction endeavors, show unseemly outrageous displeasure, or have repeating sensations of void.

3. **<u>Subordinate behavioral condition/Dependent personality disorder</u>**: an example of waiting to be dealt with and compliant and tenacious direct. Individuals with a reliant behavioral condition might experience issues settling on day-to-day choices without support from others or may feel awkward or frail while alone in light of

the stress of being unable to deal with themselves.

4. **<u>Dramatic behavioral condition/Histrionic personality disorder</u>**: an example of extreme inclination and consideration chasing. Individuals with a dramatic behavioral condition might feel awkward when they are not the focal point of consideration, may take advantage of actual appearance to focus on themselves, or have quickly fluctuating or overstated feelings.

5. **<u>Self-centered behavioral condition/Narcissistic personality disorder</u>**: an example of interest in hero worship and absence of compassion for other people. An individual with an egotistical behavioral condition might have a gaudy identity significance, a

propensity for narcissism, exploit individuals, or need sympathy.

6. **<u>Fanatical enthusiastic behavioral condition/Obsessive-compulsive personality disorder</u>**: an example of fixation on efficiency, flawlessness, and control. An individual with a fanatical enthusiastic behavioral condition might be very centered around subtleties or schedules, may work unnecessarily and not permit time for relaxation or companions, or might be unbendable in their ethical quality and goals. (This isn't equivalent to a fanatical enthusiastic problem.)

7. **<u>Jumpy behavioral condition/Paranoid personality disorder</u>**: an inclination to be skeptical of individuals and see them as brutal or resentful. Individuals with neurotic behavioral conditions by and

large accept individuals will hurt or delude them and don't trust others or foster near them.

8. **<u>Schizoid behavioral condition</u>**: being taken out from social ties and showing an insignificant inclination. An individual with a schizoid behavioral condition frequently doesn't need profound connections, decides to be separated from everyone else, and appears to not think often about commendation or analysis from others.

9. **<u>Schizotypal behavioral condition</u>**: an example of being entirely awkward in cozy connections, having distorted thinking, and strange direct. An individual with a schizotypal behavioral condition might have strange perspectives or odd or exceptional lead or discourse or

may have outrageous social nervousness.

Determination of a behavioral condition needs an emotional well-being master to check out long-haul examples of working and side effects. The analysis is normally made on grown-ups 18 or more seasoned. Individuals under 18 are frequently not determined to have behavioral conditions because their characters are as yet developing. Certain individuals with character issues may not see an issue. Likewise, people might have more than one behavioral condition. An expected 9 percent of U.S. people have something like one behavioral condition.

Treatment
Specific kinds of psychotherapy are advantageous for treating behavioral conditions. During psychotherapy, an

individual can acquire understanding and information about the turmoil and what is adding to side effects and can discuss contemplations, sentiments, and ways of behaving. Psychotherapy can assist an individual with figuring out the impacts of their conduct on others and figure out how to oversee or adapt to side effects and lessen ways of behaving bringing on some issues with working and connections. The kind of treatment will rely upon the particular behavioral condition, how serious it is, and the singular's conditions.

Usually used kinds of psychotherapy include:

- Psychoanalytic/psychodynamic treatment

- Persuasive conduct treatment

- Mental social treatment

- Bunch treatment

- Psychoeducation (showing the individual and relatives the condition, treatment, and methods of adapting) (showing the individual and relatives the ailment, treatment, and approaches to adapting)

There are no medications explicitly to treat behavioral conditions. Nonetheless, medication, like antidepressants, against nervousness medicine, or temperament settling prescription, might help tend to certain side effects. More serious or long-haul side effects might require a group treatment containing an essential consideration specialist, a therapist, a clinician, a social laborer, and relatives.

As well as effectively taking part in a treatment plan, some taking care of oneself and survival methods can be valuable for those with behavioral conditions. For example,

Finding out about the condition. Information and understanding can help engage and energize.

Getting dynamic. Actual work and exercise can assist with overseeing numerous side effects, like sadness, stress, and nervousness.

Staying away from medications and liquor. Liquor and unlawful medications could irritate side effects or associate with solutions.

Getting typical clinical consideration. Not disregarding tests or normal consideration from your essential specialist.

Joining a care group of others with character issues.

Writing in a diary to convey feelings.

Attempting to unwind and stress the executive's practices like yoga and contemplation.

Remaining associated with loved ones; trying not to get disengaged.

Relatives can be pivotal in a singular's recovery and can work with the singular's medical care supplier on the best ways of aiding and supporting. Be that as it may, having a relative with a behavioral condition can likewise be startling and unpleasant. Relatives might profit from examining with a psychological wellness expert who can furnish assistance in adapting to difficulties.

Chapter 2

Avoidant Behavioral condition

Avoidant behavioral condition is set apart by unfortunate confidence and a serious feeling of dread toward dismissal. Individuals with the condition frequently keep away from social circumstances to keep away from these sentiments. Avoidant behavioral conditions are treatable with psychotherapy (talk treatment). Prescription might help too.

What is an avoidant behavioral condition?

Avoidant behavioral condition (AVPD) is a psychological wellness condition that includes ongoing insecurities and outrageous aversion to analysis. Individuals with AVPD might want to cooperate with others, however, they will generally stay away from social communications because of their extraordinary apprehension about dismissal.

AVPD is one of a gathering of conditions called "Group C" behavioral conditions. They include uneasiness and dread. Behavioral conditions are enduring examples of conduct that are withdrawn from social standards (how we're supposed to act) and fostered in youth or puberty. They cause trouble for the individual with the condition as well as the people around them.

What's the contrast between avoidant behavioral conditions and social tension?

Avoidant behavioral conditions and social nervousness issues (Miserable) share comparative highlights and ways of

behaving. In any case, they're unmistakable circumstances.
Social uneasiness problem (social fear) happens when you have an extraordinary and continuous feeling of dread toward being judged and watched by others. This leads individuals with Miserable to stay away from social circumstances.

Individuals with AVPD likewise keep away from social circumstances and connections. Yet, it has more to do with their low confidence than with tension. Uneasiness is the center component behind Miserable, yet it doesn't need to be available with AVPD.

Specialists once felt that AVPD was a serious type of Miserable. In any case, concentrates on showing that around 66% of individuals with AVPD don't satisfy the guideline analytic standards for Miserable as per the DSM-5.
In any case, an individual can have both AVPD and Miserable. Individuals with the

two circumstances have more extreme side effects than those with only one.

How normal is an avoidant behavioral condition?
Specialists gauge that around 1.5% to 2.5% of the U.S. populace has avoidant behavioral conditions.

Who does avoidant behavioral condition influence?

Avoidant behavioral condition normally starts in your late youngsters or mid-20s. AVPD is additionally bound to influence individuals with any of the accompanying psychological wellness conditions:

- Clinical discouragement (significant burdensome issue).
- Persevering burdensome issues.
- Social uneasiness problem.
- Fanatical impulsive issue.
- Alarm jumble.

- Anorexia nervosa.
- Pigging out jumble.
- Side Effects and Causes

An avoidant behavioral condition is a psychological wellness condition that includes ongoing insecurities and outrageous aversion to analysis.

What are the side effects of avoidant behavioral conditions?

The fundamental indication of avoidant behavioral condition is having such areas of strength for dismissal that you pick confinement over being around individuals. This example of conduct can change from gentle to outrageous.

Different signs and ways of behaving of avoidant behavioral conditions include:
- Having an unfortunate mental self-portrait, considering themselves to be lacking and substandard.

- Being excessively worried about analysis or objection.

- Might be hesitant to become engaged with others except if they realize without a doubt that others will like them.

- Encountering outrageous tension (apprehension) and dread in group environments and connections. This might lead them to keep away from exercises or occupations that include being with others.

- Being modest and hesitant in friendly circumstances because of an apprehension about accomplishing something wrong or feeling humiliated.

- Tending to overstate expected issues or confuse criticism as negative.

- Rarely having a go at anything new or taking risks.

What causes avoidant behavioral conditions?

Behavioral conditions, including AVPD, are among the most un-comprehended psychological well-being conditions. Specialists are as yet attempting to sort out the reason behind them, yet they think AVPD are because of a few elements, including:

Hereditary qualities: One concentrate on AVPD assessed that hereditary qualities represent around 64% of the probability of creating AVPD.

Demeanor during earliest stages: Scientists have tracked down associations between specific personality qualities during the outset of 9500 and AVPD. They incorporate inflexibility, touchiness, not seeking after new encounters, keeping away from conceivable mischief more than expected, and extreme apprehension and pain.

Connection style: Individuals with an unfortunate connection style might be bound to foster AVPD. An unfortunate connection style implies you want closeness with others however have doubt in them and a feeling of dread toward dismissal. This connection style can create, for instance, if a negligibly expressive baby shows trouble and their parental figure is contemptuous.

Youth climate: Encountering dismissal and being dealt with uniquely in contrast to others during adolescence might add to the advancement of AVPD.

Analysis and Tests

How is avoidant behavioral condition analyzed?

Character keeps on advancing all through youngster and juvenile turn of events. Along these lines, medical services suppliers don't ordinarily determine somebody to have an avoidant behavioral condition until after the age of 18. Suppliers need proof that these examples of conduct are persevering and resolute and don't blur with time.

Behavioral conditions, including avoidant behavioral conditions, can be hard to analyze. This is because the vast majority one don't believe there's an issue with their way of behaving or perspective.
At the point when they do look for help, it's frequently because of conditions, for example, tension or discouragement from the issues made by their behavioral condition, similar to separation or solitude.

At the point when emotional wellness proficient, for example, a clinician or specialist, suspects somebody could have the avoidant behavioral condition, they frequently ask expansive, general inquiries that will not establish a climate that the individual could consider basic or humiliating. They pose inquiries that will reveal insight into:
- Previous history.
- Connections.
- Past work history.
- Reality testing.

An individual associated with having avoidant behavioral conditions might need an understanding of their ways of behaving and thought designs. In this way, psychological well-being experts frequently work with the individual's loved ones to gather more data about their ways of behaving and history.

Emotional well-being suppliers base a determination of avoidant behavioral conditions on the models for the condition in the American Mental Affiliation's Symptomatic and Measurable Manual of Mental Issues (DSM-5).

Demonstrative measures for avoidant behavioral conditions include a constant example of no less than four of the accompanying ways of behaving:

- Keep away from work-related exercises that include working with others since they dread that others will scrutinize or dismiss them.

- Being reluctant to engage with others except if they're certain others will like them.

- They are detached or saved in cozy connections since they dread criticism or embarrassment.

- Intense stress over others censuring or dismissing them in standard social circumstances.

- Feeling hesitant in new friendly circumstances since they feel deficient.

- Surveying themselves as socially untalented, unappealing, or sub-par compared to other people.

- They are hesitant to face individual challenges or attempt new exercises since they might feel humiliated.

The board and Treatment

What is the treatment for avoidant behavioral conditions?

Treating behavioral conditions is troublesome because individuals with these circumstances have well-established thought processes and conduct that have existed for a long time.

Notwithstanding, individuals with avoidant behavioral conditions will generally be a great possibility for treatment because the condition causes them huge pain. Also, the vast majority with AVPD need to foster connections. This want can be a rousing element for individuals with AVPD to follow their treatment plans, which will probably incorporate psychotherapy and, possibly, prescription.

Treatment for individuals with this condition is best when relatives are involved and strong.

Psychotherapy for AVPD

Psychotherapy (talk treatment) is the treatment of decisions for behavioral conditions. The objective of treatment is to assist you with uncovering the inspirations and fears related to your viewpoints and conduct. Also, you can figure out how to decidedly connect with others more.

Two explicit kinds of psychotherapy that can assist individuals with AVPD include:

- ***Psychodynamic treatment***: This kind of treatment centers around the mental foundations of close-to-home misery. Through self-reflection, you investigate tricky connections and ways of behaving in your life. This assists you with better grasping yourself. It can assist you with changing how you connect with others and your current circumstances.

- ***Mental conduct treatment (CBT):*** This is an organized, objective-situated kind of treatment. A specialist or therapist assists you with investigating your contemplations and feelings. You'll come to comprehend what your contemplations mean for your activities. Through CBT, you can forget negative contemplations and ways of behaving. You'll figure out how to embrace better reasoning examples and propensities. It might particularly zero in on creating interactive abilities.

Drug for AVPD

There's at present no drug that can treat behavioral conditions. Yet, there's medicine for sorrow and nervousness, which individuals with avoidant behavioral conditions may likewise have. Treating these circumstances can make it more straightforward to treat AVPD.

For the best outcomes, in any case, you ought to take medicine mixed with psychotherapy.

Anticipation

Will the avoidant behavioral condition be forestalled?

You can't forestall avoidant behavioral conditions. Be that as it may, treatment can assist with diminishing the issues it causes. Looking for help when side effects seem can assist with diminishing the interruption to the individual's life, family, and fellowships.

Standpoint

What is the visualization for individuals with avoidant behavioral conditions?

The visualization (viewpoint) for AVPD relies upon the event that it's dealt with or not.

Left untreated, AVPD might result in:

- Extra psychological wellness conditions, similar to despondency, substance use confusion, and dietary issues.
- Expanded hazard of post-birth anxiety.
- Disappointment with life.
- Work hardships.
- Hindered social working.

- Individuals with AVPD likewise experience higher paces of self-destructive ideation and self-destruction endeavors.

Treatment for avoidant behavioral conditions is a long interaction. Your readiness to look for and remain with treatment can essentially affect your standpoint. With treatment, certain individuals with AVPD can figure out how to strongly connect with others more.

A Significant Note

It's memorable's critical that avoidant behavioral condition (AVPD) is an emotional well-being condition. Similarly as with all emotional wellness conditions, looking for help when side effects seem can assist with diminishing the disturbances to your life. Psychological wellness experts can offer treatment designs that can assist you with dealing with your viewpoints and ways of behaving.

The friends and family of individuals with AVPD frequently experience pressure, melancholy, and confinement. It's critical to deal with your emotional wellness and look for help assuming that you're encountering these side effects.

Chapter 3

An Aide for Accomplices/Friends and family of Individuals With Avoidant Behavioral conditions

Avoidant behavioral condition (AVPD) will spread the word about its presence in an individual's connections, and if left neglected and unacknowledged it can pressure those connections to the limit. Be that as it may, individuals who love the people who have this unavoidable condition can assume a crucial part in their possible recuperation, by offering them acknowledgment and understanding and by supporting their endeavors to change with generosity, responsiveness, and sympathy.

According to the point of view of the individuals who esteem them, the way of behaving of individuals with avoidant behavioral conditions can appear to be confusing. You know your cherished one with AVPD as a warm, touchy, and kind individual who can be clever and charming when they're with others they know personally and trust.

However, when they're in the organization of new individuals, or those they just know nonchalantly, they can abruptly close down. They become exorbitantly peaceful, as their non-verbal communication and looks uncover a degree of stress and nervousness that appears to be improper to the circumstance.

On the off chance that you're involved with somebody who has AVPD, you probably value their delicacy and liberality. Be that as it may, you might struggle with understanding the reason why they can't show those characteristics constantly, to others other than you and a couple of dear companions or relatives.

Sadly, this is the effect of avoidant behavioral conditions, uncovering itself straightforwardly. AVPD is a life-changing condition, and it carries distress and battle to the existence of the individuals who should manage it consistently.

Fortunately, individuals with AVPD are continually looking for answers to the difficulties and dissatisfactions their condition makes. They need to be perceived and acknowledged for what their identity is, however they additionally need to develop and advance.

Avoidant Behavioral condition and the Weakening Anxiety toward Dismissal
The social troubles of people with avoidant behavioral conditions can be followed by a significant and firmly established apprehension about being judged, censured,

and dismissed. In the organization of others, they feel vigorously examined and are many times persuaded that others can recognize their uneasiness or social awkwardness and are making a decision about them brutally for it. Their overpowering social tension is a sign of their battles with constantly low confidence, which leaves them regularly questioning their value and worth.

Individuals with AVPD know about these issues, and somewhat they realize their uncertainties are nonsensical. In any case, realizing this isn't sufficient to make the reluctance disappear. Their deep-seated insecurities and mediocrity are imbued, and it can require numerous long stretches of treatment, self-reflection, and other certainty and confidence-building systems before their most terrible AVPD side effects start to decrease in strength and impact.

At last, their excursion to health is one they should finish all alone. However, you can assist them with arriving at their objectives and accomplish a degree of self-acknowledgment that makes those objectives reasonable.

Strengthening through Approval
What your band together with avoidant behavioral conditions will expect from you, in particular, is approval. They need to realize that you comprehend their battles are genuine and have caused them much agony all through their lives.

You ought to urge them to talk transparently and truly about their sentiments and encounters. Tell them you are prepared to be their protected harbor, so they realize they can uncover their most profound apprehensions and greatest frustrations to you unafraid of being judged or dismissed.

As you hear their words, you ought to ensure you're truly tuning in and retaining what they're talking about. You'll acquire a firmer handle on how AVPD works and learn significantly more about how it twists mindfulness and an individual's view of the world.

Another way you can offer approval is by telling them you understand areas of strength for how required to have been to make due, and that you regard them for their boldness.

AVPD is a persevering condition that can influence practically every part of an individual's life, and that implies the people who have it should track down ways of pushing ahead notwithstanding its unavoidable, day-to-day influence. AVPD makes life more dangerous than it ought to be, yet people with avoidant behavioral conditions keep on attempting to work on their lives, and as they endeavor to adapt to their side effects as well as they probably are aware of how.

Your relationship, and the existence you two have been endeavoring to fabricate together, is in some measure to a limited extent a consequence of your cherished one's assurance to not allow their AVPD to obliterate their fantasies. Your accomplice is equipped to achieve a ton, particularly if their endeavors are upheld and supported by the people who care about them most.

Making New Powers of Profound Devotion and Backing

While there are special cases, generally individuals with AVPD will not have many close or personal connections with more distant family individuals, colleagues, neighbors, and other people who are in their circles yet not in similar vicinity as accomplices, guardians, kids, kin, or long-lasting companions. Furthermore, people who battle to interface with their more distant family won't make some simple memories holding or associating with the individuals from your family, who are near you however far off from them.

Assuming you attempt to make such bonds by tossing your cherished one along with your relatives at parties, special festivals, or close family meals, you're probably going to be frustrated with the result. Also, you'll put your accomplice under pressure, pushing them into a circumstance that nearly appears to be intended to cause them to feel awkward.
It's ideal to treat your assumptions regarding such things early, by recognizing that the ordinary guidelines about how to unite individuals will not matter in this case.

The best way to overcome any barrier that keeps individuals with AVPD from extending their groups of friends is to take things gradually and continuously, and with practically no assumption that new associations will be made rapidly or naturally.

Your cherished one can effectively be incorporated into your more extensive organization of loved ones after some time. In any case, that will possibly occur assuming you let the cycle progress at a speed that keeps your accomplice from feeling worried or pushed, or judged if their social presentation doesn't satisfy foreordained principles. You ought to converse with your relatives and companions somewhat early and let them in that it requires investment for your accomplice to figure out how to trust, which is important before they can start to give down their gatekeeper and let others access.

From Little Triumphs Come Significant Triumphs

At the point when you comprehend how unequivocally and instinctually unfortunate an individual with an avoidant behavioral condition is tied in with being judged, condemned, dismissed, overlooked, giggled at, or humiliated, you'll have the option to appreciate and recognize their little victories — which, according to their viewpoint, aren't little in any way.

For an individual with AVPD, a social outcome of any sort might address a huge forward leap. Straightforward cooperation that others underestimate can appear to be amazingly unsafe and questionable for them, and when they figure out how to push through their feelings of trepidation and talk or connect, it addresses a legitimate achievement that ought to be built up with good input.

Alternately, if and when they experience disappointment, because their weaknesses outwitted them, you ought to be comparably certain and empowering. Tell them you understand the amount they battle to communicate for themselves or advocate for themselves now and again. Assist them with seeing their mistake are just brief misfortunes, and that every little disappointment can be a forerunner to greater achievement later on.

Treatment for Avoidant Behavioral Condition

Individuals will generally consider behavioral conditions a sort of design that can't be changed.

In any case, this mistaken supposition. At the point when people with behavioral conditions see their circumstances as risky and are focused on giving their maximum effort to change and recuperate, they can gain extraordinary headway throughout a serious, long-haul treatment plan.

This is particularly evident with avoidant behavioral conditions, since the people who have it encounter long periods of dissatisfaction, disappointment, depression, and underachievement. They retreat socially and genuinely because they feel like they need to, not because they need to. On the off chance that they are persuaded treatment will have an effect, they will put forth a coordinated attempt to embrace the open door.

Short-term and private treatment projects can both be successful against avoidant behavioral conditions. Nonetheless, assuming your accomplice has fostered extra emotional wellness issues (like despondency or uneasiness problems) or substance use issues, the ongoing methodology is certainly ideal.

It very well may be a battle for individuals with AVPD to open up to emotional well-being experts. Their social uneasiness and apprehension about being judged can be an impediment even with individuals who are attempting to help them, in any event, when the environment is modified to create recuperating and recuperation.

Therefore, your accomplice's possibility of rising out of treatment feeling better and enabled will decisively increase if you and other people who care about them partake in your cherished one's recuperation program. You can offer essential close-to-home and moral help in family treatment meetings, and during normal visits when they are permitted. You ought to likewise remain nearby with the individuals from your cherished one's treatment group, to hear progress reports and get master counsel.

Your committed and steady contribution in their recuperation can give your accomplice the sort of uplifting feedback and encouragement.